From Graduation to Elevation:

Your Guide to Landing & Loving Your First Job

MAC BELENZO, CHRA

DEDICATION

To the dreamers, the doers, and those standing on the threshold of greatness: the fresh graduates. May you find your path, make your mark, and elevate from lessons learned and challenges met. Remember, every ending is a new beginning. As one chapter closes, let this guide light the way for the story you're about to write in the world of professionalism. To all the mentors, educators, and families who've shaped and supported these graduates — this is a salute to your unwavering belief.

CONTENTS

ACKNOWLEDGMENTS

Writing this book has been a journey, not one I have taken alone. There have been guides, mentors, well-wishers, and silent supporters every step of the way. As I present this work to my fellow countrymen, and to the world, it is only fitting to express my deepest gratitude to everyone who has been a part of this incredible voyage.

First and foremost, I extend my heartfelt thanks to all the fresh graduates, jobseekers, and future graduates. Your aspirations, challenges, and relentless spirit have been the bedrock upon which this book is built. Your stories and experiences provided both direction and inspiration.

I owe immense gratitude to all my past interviewers and supervisors who have shaped my perspectives and enriched this book's content. Special thanks to Ms. Raquel from San Beda; Ms. Joan and Sir Jeff from FEU; Ms. Aubs, Ms. Marleth, and Ms. Jace from Ateneo-CCE; Ms. Jam, Ms. Mindy, Ms. Jane, and Ms. Joanne from Gerry's; and Ms. Che, Ms. Kate, and Fr. Lao from UST-Legazpi. The diverse interviewing styles and unique approaches I have experienced with each of you have been a deep source of inspiration. These experiences, combined with the foundational principles of HRDM and I/O Psychology, greatly influenced this book's content.

A special mention to my family, especially to my wife, Jane and my daughter, Sophia whose unwavering support and belief in this project provided the motivation to push through the late nights and challenging moments. You have been my anchor throughout.

To my friends, for the constant encouragement, and for always being there, and to those who have shared their success stories with me – thank you.

Lastly, to you, dear reader. This book is for you and because of you. Thank you for embarking on this journey with me. I hope the insights and strategies in these pages serve you well as you navigate the vibrant job market.

Maraming salamat. Onwards to greater success!

INTRODUCTION

In the heart of the bustling streets of Manila, lies a common thread that binds every fresh graduate: the dream of making a mark in the world of work. Yet, as you stand on the brink of this new chapter, the path forward might seem riddled with questions: How do I craft a resume that speaks volumes? What are employers truly seeking during interviews? How do I turn my probationary role into a stable, fulfilling career?

Welcome to your compass for the Filipino job market – a guide designed to illuminate your path, blending the unique cultural nuances with universally acclaimed professional practices. You're not just holding a book; you're cradling a toolkit. Within these pages, you'll find not just tips, but tried-and-tested strategies and insights rooted in the intricacies of the local job market. Whether you're navigating the corporate skyscrapers of Makati or the dynamic start-ups of Bonifacio Global City, the wisdom herein is tailored to the aspirations and challenges of young professionals like you.

By the end of this guide, you won't just be equipped with knowledge; you'll be empowered with confidence. Confidence to craft compelling resumes, ace interviews, and shine bright in the workplace, all while staying true to the values and spirit that make us uniquely Filipino.

"Tara na!" Let's embark on this journey together and unlock the doors to your   professional   future.

CHAPTER 1:
UNDERSTANDING THE JOB MARKET

Stepping out of the academic world and into the professional realm can be both exhilarating and daunting. You are not just transitioning into a new phase of life; you are venturing into a vast, dynamic, and often unpredictable landscape: the job market. Understanding this market is the first crucial step in carving a niche for yourself and setting the trajectory for a fulfilling career.

The job market, much like any market, operates on the principles of demand and supply. It is a place where employers search for the right talent, and job seekers strive to find roles that align with their skills, passions, and career aspirations. But it is not as straightforward as it sounds. Economic factors, technological advancements, socio-political changes, and now, even global health scenarios, play a crucial role in shaping its dynamics.

In the Philippines, the job market is further nuanced by our rich cultural heritage, values, and the ever-evolving local industries. From the booming BPO sector and the rise of startups to the traditional corporate giants and the promising digital economy, the opportunities are vast, but so are the challenges.

This chapter aims to demystify the intricacies of the job market for you. By the end, you will have a holistic view of the prevailing trends, the sectors that are on the rise, the skills most in demand, and the challenges you might face. Equipped with this knowledge, you'll be better prepared to navigate your career journey with confidence and clarity.

So, let us embark on this exploration and lay the foundation for your professional voyage.

OVERVIEW OF POPULAR INDUSTRIES FOR FRESH GRADUATES

1. **Business Process Outsourcing (BPO)**
   The BPO sector has remained a significant employer for fresh graduates for years. Whether in customer service, technical support, or back-end office roles, BPOs often offer attractive compensation packages and opportunities for quick career growth.

2. **Information Technology (IT) and Software Development**
   With the rise of tech startups and the digital transformation of traditional businesses, there is a growing demand for software engineers, IT specialists, and digital marketers.

3. **Tourism and Hospitality**
   The Philippines, being an archipelago with stunning beaches and destinations, has a robust tourism industry. Graduates from hotel and restaurant management, tourism, and related courses often find opportunities in this sector.

4. **Banking and Finance**
   From traditional banking roles to fintech startups, there's a continuous demand for finance and economics graduates in this sector.

5. **Healthcare**
   With nursing being one of the staple courses in many universities, there's always a demand both locally and internationally for healthcare professionals.

6. **Education and Training**
   The demand for educators, especially for the K-12 program and the private tutoring sector, continues to grow, providing opportunities for education graduates.

TYPICAL JOB APPLICATION PROCESS AND TIMELINE

1. **Job Search and Application**
   Graduates typically begin by searching for positions on job portals, company websites, or through referrals. This can take anywhere from a few days to several weeks or even months, depending on the industry and specific roles.

2. **Initial Screening**
   Once an application is sent, HR departments typically take a week or two to screen resumes. Shortlisted candidates are then contacted for the next steps.

3. **Assessment and Examinations**
   Depending on the role and company, applicants may be asked to undergo aptitude or technical exams. This stage can take a day to a week.

4. **Interviews**
   This usually involves multiple rounds, starting from HR and moving up to department heads or team leaders. Each interview can be spaced days or even weeks apart.

5. **Job Offer**
   After successful interviews, candidates receive a job offer, which they can either accept or negotiate. This can take a week after the final interview.

6. **Onboarding**
   Once an offer is accepted, candidates undergo orientation and training. This can range from a few days to several weeks, depending on the complexity of the role.

PROBATIONARY EMPLOYMENT

It is common practice for companies to hire new employees on a probationary basis. This period allows employers to evaluate a new hire's performance, skills, and fit within the company culture.

1. **Duration**
   The probationary period usually lasts for six months, though it can be shorter depending on the company and the role.

2. **Performance Evaluation**
   Towards the end of the probationary period, the employee undergoes a performance evaluation to determine if they'll be regularized or if their employment will be terminated.

3. **Rights of Probationary Employees**
   Even during probation, employees are entitled to the same rights as regular employees, such as receiving the minimum wage, benefits, and holiday pay. However, they might not be eligible for some company-specific perks until they achieve regular status.

4. **Regularization**
   If an employee's performance meets or exceeds expectations, they are then "regularized," granting them more job security and often additional benefits.

CHAPTER 2:
CRAFTING YOUR FIRST RESUME

BASICS OF RESUME WRITING

1. **Personal Information**

   The personal information section is the gateway to your resume. Think of it as the front porch of a house. Before anyone enters, they will first see and assess the exterior. Your personal details set the first impression, so it is essential to get it right.

   a. **Name**

      It is the most prominent identifier and the first thing employers see.

      Tips:
      - Use your full legal name (based on the name provided on your valid IDs and/or PSA/NSO birth certificate). Avoid nicknames or diminutives unless they are widely recognized in professional circles.

      - Consider bolding or using a slightly larger font size for your name to make it stand out.

   b. **Contact Information:**

      - **Mobile Number.** Employers might reach out via a call or text for interview scheduling or clarifications.

      Tips:
      - Ensure the number is active and you answer it professionally.
      - Mentioning the country code (e.g., +63 for the Philippines) can be useful if applying for roles in multinational companies or if there is a chance the hiring manager is outside the country.

- **Email Address**

  Most formal communications, like interview invites or job offers, are sent via email.

  Tips:
  - Use a professional email address, preferably a combination of your first and last name. Avoid quirky addresses like *"sweetiepie123@email.com."*

  - Stick to widely recognized email providers like Gmail, Outlook, or Yahoo for better deliverability.

c. **Address**

This helps employers know your general location, which can be relevant for logistical reasons.

Tips:
- For security and privacy reasons, it is often sufficient to mention only the city or municipality and the province, especially for jobs where the specific location is not crucial.

- If applying internationally, include the country in the address.

d. **Date of Birth**

This is often optional and, in some countries, not recommended due to age discrimination concerns. If it is customary in your industry or region, you can include it. Otherwise, consider leaving it out.

e. **Civil Status**

Like the date of birth, including civil status is not a universal norm. Only provide this if it is a common practice in your country or industry.

Final Tips

- Ensure your contact details are consistent across all job application materials, including your resume, cover letter, and any online profiles.

- Remember, your resume may be seen by multiple people during the hiring process. Only provide information you are comfortable sharing widely.

- Keep the position you are applying for in mind. Tailor the personal information section to what is most relevant and expected for that role and industry.

In essence, the personal information on your resume is more than just a list of details. It is an opportunity to set the tone and make a strong first impression, so it's worth taking the time to perfect it.

2. **Objective/Summary**

The resume's Objective or Summary section offers a snapshot of your career aspirations and qualifications, providing employers with an immediate sense of who you are and what you bring to the table. While they have different focuses, both serve as an "elevator pitch" for your professional persona.

A. **Objective**

The objective statement clearly states what you are seeking in terms of employment and how it aligns with your career goals.

When to Use:
- You are a fresh graduate or an entry-level applicant.
- You are shifting industries or roles.

- The job you're applying for requires a specific focus.

Tips:

- If you are applying for a marketing role, mention it. E.g., *"Seeking a marketing position to leverage my skills in digital advertising and content creation."*

- Your objective should resonate with the role you're applying for.

- Ideally, it should be no more than 2 sentences.

- Highlight how the employer will benefit from hiring you.

Example:

"Recent communications graduate seeking a public relations role to leverage my skills in media relations and content creation, aiming to boost brand awareness and engagement."

B. Summary

The summary (sometimes termed a "Professional Summary" or "Resume Profile") provides a brief overview of your qualifications, skills, and achievements, presenting a condensed version of your professional story.

When to Use:

- You have a substantial amount of experience in the field.

- Your career trajectory shows a clear and specific focus.

- The resume might be longer, and you want to immediately highlight key points.

Tips:

- Mention any significant milestones or accomplishments that make you a standout candidate.

- Use terms that are relevant to the industry and the specific job role.

- If possible, include numbers. E.g., *"Boosted sales by 30% in Q1 2022."*

- Aim for 3-4 impactful sentences.

Example:
"Digital marketing manager with over 5 years of experience specializing in e-commerce platforms. Proven track record of increasing organic traffic by 40% and enhancing conversion rates through targeted campaigns. Adept at leveraging SEO, PPC, and content strategies."

Objective vs. Summary

While both sections cannot typically coexist on a resume due to redundancy, choose the one that best matches your current career stage and the job you're applying for.

Remember that hiring managers often skim resumes, especially when they have a large pile to go through. An impactful Objective or Summary can quickly grab their attention, making them want to delve deeper into the rest of your document. This section, while brief, is your chance to make a compelling first impression. Craft it with care, ensuring it encapsulates your professional essence effectively.

3. **Education**
   The Education section of a resume provides prospective employers with insights into your academic qualifications and achievements. For many roles, especially entry-level positions and professions requiring specific credentials, your educational background is a

significant factor in the hiring decision. Here's how to optimally present this section:

Basics of Listing Education

a. **School Name and Location**
Always include the name of the institution where you studied.

Specify the city and country, especially if it is an international school or if the job you're applying for is abroad.

b. **Degree Obtained**
Mention the full title of the degree. E.g., *"Bachelor of Science in Computer Engineering"* or *"Master of Arts in Communication."*

c. **Major/Minor or Specialization**
If applicable, specify your major or any specializations. This can be especially relevant for positions that require expertise in a particular area.

d. **Graduation Date**
Mention the month and year of your graduation. If you're still a student, you can list the expected graduation date.

e. **Relevant Coursework**
For fresh graduates or those applying to positions where specific courses are advantageous, listing a few key courses can be beneficial.

f. **Honors and Achievements**
Include academic honors like *"cum laude"* or *"dean's list."*
Scholarships, awards, or any notable academic achievements can also be listed.

Additional Tips & Considerations:

a. Always list your educational experiences in reverse chronological order, starting with the most recent.

b. Include your GPA if it is strong and if it is a common practice in your industry.

c. If you have completed a significant project or thesis, especially if it is relevant to the job, consider adding a brief description or title.

d. For roles where vocational training or certificates are crucial (like IT certifications or first-aid courses), these can be listed either under the Education section or in a separate "Certifications" section, depending on their importance.

e. Typically, once you have obtained a college or university degree, high school education can be omitted unless you are a very recent graduate, or it is customary to include it in your region.

Tailoring for Market

a. **Licensure Exams**
   If you have passed a board or licensure (like the Bar for lawyers or the board exam for psychometricians/psychologists), it is crucial to include this, as it is a significant credential.

b. **Local University Recognition**
   If you graduated from a well-known university like UP, Ateneo, La Salle, or UST, the institution's reputation could be a notable point in your favor, given the recognition these universities have locally.

Your Education section is more than just a chronicle of your academic history. It is a testament to your foundational knowledge, dedication, and achievements in a structured learning environment. Especially for those early in their careers, this section can significantly influence an employer's perception and decision. Ensure it is comprehensive, accurate, and tailored to the position for which you're applying.

4. **Work Experience (if any)**

The Work Experience section of your resume is often the most scrutinized part by potential employers. It chronicles your professional journey, highlighting roles you've undertaken, responsibilities you've managed, and achievements you've garnered in the workplace.

Basics of Listing Work Experience

a. Job Title:
- Clearly state your official job title.

- If you hold multiple roles within the same company, list each title separately to demonstrate progression.

b. Company Name and Location:
- Specify the full name of the company or organization where you worked.

- Include the city and, if relevant, the country of the company's location, especially if you have worked abroad or are applying for international roles.

c. Employment Duration:
- Clearly list the start and end dates of your employment in each position. Typically, this is formatted as month/year – month/year (e.g., *"June 2019 – May 2021"*).

d. Job Responsibilities:
- Provide a concise list or brief descriptions of the primary tasks, responsibilities, and roles you undertook.

- Use action verbs to start each point, like *"Managed," "Coordinated," "Designed,"* etc.

e. Achievements and Accomplishments:
- Beyond responsibilities, highlight any notable achievements.

- Whenever possible, quantify these points, e.g., *"Increased sales by 15% in the first quarter"* or *"Led a team of 10 to complete project X under budget."*

Additional Tips & Considerations:

a. List your roles starting with the most recent and working backward. This format lets employers see your current or latest role first.

b. Emphasize experiences and responsibilities that are most relevant to the job you're applying for.

c. Bullet points make your resume more reader-friendly and allow employers to quickly scan through your responsibilities and achievements.

d. While industry-specific terms might be understood by experts in your field, remember that the first person to see your resume might be an HR specialist unfamiliar with niche terminologies.

e. Especially for fresh graduates or those with limited work experience, internships, part-time roles, and volunteer positions can be valuable in demonstrating skills and commitment.

f. It is generally not necessary to include reasons for leaving a job on your resume. This topic may come up in interviews, so be prepared to discuss it there.

g. If you have significant gaps in your employment history, be ready to explain them in an interview. Some people also use a cover letter to address any large gaps.

Tailoring for Different Career Stages

a. **Entry-Level or Fresh Graduates:**

- Focus on internships, part-time jobs, volunteer experiences, and even major academic projects.

- Emphasize transferable skills, like teamwork, leadership, or communication.

b. Mid-Career Professionals:

- Highlight achievements and outcomes, not just responsibilities.

- Remove older roles that are no longer as relevant, especially if you've been in the workforce for over 10-15 years.

c. Senior Professionals or Executives:

- Emphasize leadership roles, major projects led, and significant impacts made on organizations.

- A summary or profile section can be valuable to immediately showcase your most notable achievements and qualifications.

The Work Experience section provides a narrative of your professional journey. Every role, responsibility, and achievement tell a story of your growth, skills, and value as an employee. Craft this section with care, ensuring it effectively communicates your professional trajectory and the unique value you can bring to a potential employer.

5. Skills

The Skills section on a resume showcases your proficiencies, abilities, and expertise, both technical and soft. Given its importance, many hiring managers will directly seek out this section to quickly gauge if you are a suitable candidate for a position.

Types of Skills:

a. Hard (Technical) Skills

These are specific and teachable abilities or knowledge sets that you've gained through education, training, or experience.

Examples: *Proficiency in a programming language, ability to use a specific machine, knowledge of a foreign language, expertise in a particular software tool.*

b. Soft Skills

These are less tangible and harder to quantify. They often pertain to how you work with others and approach your job.

Examples: *Communication, teamwork, problem-solving, adaptability, leadership.*

c. Transferable Skills.

These are abilities you have honed in one setting (e.g., a past job or university) that can be applied to various roles or industries.

Examples: *Time management, analytical thinking, public speaking.*

Organizing the Skills Section

a. Categorization:

- For resumes with a wide array of skills, consider grouping them into categories for clarity.

  Example categories:
  Technical Skills, Language Proficiencies, Leadership & Management, Software & Tools.

b. Prioritization:

- List the most relevant skills for the job you are applying for at the beginning of the section.

- Match your skills with the requirements listed in the job description.

c. Formatting:

- Use bullet points for easy readability.

- Avoid large paragraphs, which can be daunting for hiring managers to skim through.

Tips for Listing Skills:

a. Instead of generic terms like *"Computer Skills,"* specify what you can do, e.g., *"Expertise in Adobe Photoshop and Illustrator."*

b. *"Fluent in Spanish"* or *"Able to type 80 words per minute."*

c. Terms like *"hard-working"* or *"team player"* can be redundant without context. Instead of listing them as skills, demonstrate them through your achievements or responsibilities in the Work Experience section.

d. Only list skills you genuinely possess. You might be tested on them during the interview process or once you're on the job.

e. If you have obtained certifications for specific skills, they can either be listed within the Skills section or under a separate *"Certifications"* section, depending on their importance.

Remember, skills evolve with the job market. It is beneficial to regularly update this section and engage in lifelong learning. Consider periodic training, workshops, courses, or self-study to acquire new skills or enhance existing ones. Sites like Coursera, Udemy, or LinkedIn Learning offer a myriad of courses on diverse topics.

The Skills section is not just a list but a testament to your versatility, adaptability, and preparedness for a role. By effectively presenting this section, you provide hiring managers with a snapshot of what you bring to the table, increasing your chances of progressing to the interview stage.

Tailor it wisely, and ensure it accurately reflects your abilities.

6. **Achievements**

   The Achievements section of your resume is a platform to showcase significant accomplishments throughout your academic and professional journey. It is an avenue to demonstrate the tangible impact you've made in your roles, setting you apart from other candidates.

Defining Achievements

Achievements are not just tasks you have done; they are notable accomplishments, often accompanied by quantifiable results or recognitions. These can stem from:

- Overcoming challenges in the workplace.
- Meeting or surpassing specific targets or metrics.
- Receiving awards or accolades.
- Implementing changes leading to positive outcomes.
- Leading important projects or initiatives.

Listing Achievements

a. **Quantify Results:**
   - Use numbers, percentages, or other metrics to highlight the impact.

   - Example: *"Increased quarterly sales by 15%, leading the team for three consecutive quarters."*

b. **Highlight Recognitions:**
   - Did you receive an *"Employee of the Month"* award? Or perhaps recognized for a pivotal role in a project? Include these accolades.

c. **Specify the Impact:**
   - Do not just state what you did; mention its significance.

- Example: *"Designed a new client feedback system leading to a 25% reduction in customer complaints."*

d. Utilize Action Verbs:

- Begin each achievement with a strong action verb.

- Examples: *"Spearheaded, Transformed, Orchestrated, Optimized."*

e. Contextualize:

- Providing context can make some achievements more impactful. This can be particularly useful when the significance of the achievement might not be immediately apparent to those outside your field or industry.

Positioning Achievements

If you have numerous notable achievements, you can dedicate a whole section to them, usually placed near the top of your resume for emphasis.

Alternatively, you can integrate achievements within your Work Experience section, listing them under the relevant positions.

For fresh graduates or those in academia, significant achievements can be mentioned in the Education section. Examples include high GPAs, honors, scholarships, or crucial projects/research.

Tips for Crafting the Achievements Section:

a. Tailor your achievements to be relevant to the position you are applying for. A hiring manager will be most interested in accomplishments that suggest you'll excel in the desired role.

b. Ensure that your achievements are clear and comprehensible to someone outside of your previous company or industry.

c. Never exaggerate or falsify achievements. Authenticity is crucial, as many employers will verify details during the interview or reference check.

Examples of Achievements:

- *"Championed the digital transformation initiative, leading to a 40% increase in online sales in a year."*

- *"Secured the 'Top Salesperson' award two years in a row among a team of 50+ individuals."*

- *"Published 3 research papers in international peer-reviewed journals on renewable energy solutions."*

- *"Reduced operational costs by 20% through the implementation of a lean management strategy."*

Achievements serve as concrete evidence of your capabilities, accomplishments, and the value you can offer to prospective employers. They bring life to your resume, transforming it from a mere list of responsibilities into a compelling narrative of your professional journey. When crafted meticulously, the Achievements section can be a powerful tool to make your resume stand out and resonate with hiring managers.

7. **References**
   References serve as external validators of your professional achievements, work ethic, and character. They can provide potential employers with insights into your performance, capabilities, and personal attributes, painting a clearer picture of what it might be like to have you as part of their team.

What are References?

Individuals who can vouch for your qualifications for a job based on their insight into your work ethic, skills, achievements, and personal character.

Types:

a. Professional References

Past or current employers, supervisors, colleagues, or even clients who can provide feedback on your job performance, achievements, and professional demeanor.

b. Personal (or Character) References

People who can vouch for your personal character and qualities, often not from a work setting, like coaches, professors, or long-term acquaintances. They are usually used when there's limited work experience.

Listing References on Your Resume

- **Separate Document**
Traditionally, references aren't listed directly on the resume. Instead, they are provided on a separate document titled "References" or provided when requested by a potential employer.

Key Information to Include:

a. Full Name
The complete name of your reference.

b. Relationship
Specify your professional relationship to the reference, e.g., *"Former Supervisor"* or *"Colleague."*

c. Company/Organization
Where the reference currently works or where you both worked together.

d. Position/Title
Your reference's current job title.

e. Contact Information

Typically, a phone number and professional email address. Occasionally, a physical address might be included, though it's less common nowadays.

f. Notes (Optional)

Any additional context that might help, such as the projects you worked on together or the duration of your working relationship.

Typical Format:

Name: Mr. Mac Aldio Belenzo, CHRA

Position: Human Resource Officer

Current Role: Department Head in Casa Ver'Amore

Contact: mbelenzo@cva.com.ph | 09123456789

Best Practices & Considerations

1. Always get permission before listing someone as a reference. This gives them a heads-up that they might be contacted and allows them to prepare.

2. Ensure your references will provide positive feedback. It is also beneficial if they are familiar with significant achievements or qualities relevant to the job you're applying for.

3. While friends might speak highly of you, it is often best to provide professional references unless specifically asked for personal ones.

4. Make sure the contact details for your references are up-to-date. It is also a good idea to touch base with them occasionally, especially if there has been a significant lapse of time since you last worked together.

5. Inform them about the position you are applying for and provide them with a copy of your resume. This helps them align their feedback with the job requirements.

6. "References Available Upon Request". This phrase was once standard at the bottom of resumes. However, it is largely considered redundant now, as employers assume you will provide references if asked. You can save space by leaving it off.

7. Always express gratitude to your references, regardless of whether you secure the position. They have taken the time to help you in your professional journey.

While the role of references in hiring processes varies across industries and regions, they remain an integral part of many recruitment practices. Effective selection and management of references can strengthen your application, providing third-party validation of your qualifications and character. Always approach the topic with professionalism, ensuring your references are well-prepared and appreciative of their support.

Tailoring Your Resume for the Market

When applying for jobs, understanding the cultural, professional, and market-specific nuances can greatly increase your chances of landing an interview. The job market has its unique attributes, preferences, and unwritten rules. Let us dive deep into crafting a resume tailored for this specific audience.

1. **Cultural Sensitivities & Norms**
   Filipinos value respect and formality, especially in professional settings. When mentioning names, using honorifics like "Mr." or "Ms." followed by the surname is typical.

   In certain contexts, familial affiliations, especially if related to known or respected entities, can be perceived as adding credibility. However, use this information judiciously and ensure it's relevant to the application.

Participation in community service, church activities, or local organizations is seen positively. It often portrays commitment, leadership, and groundedness.

2. **Format & Presentation**
   For fresh graduates or those with fewer years of experience, a one-page resume is standard. Mid-level professionals might stretch to two pages. However, unlike some western markets, longer resumes are sometimes acceptable for senior roles, particularly if detailing significant projects or achievements.

   While not mandatory, some Filipino employers expect a 2x2 or passport-sized photo to be included in the resume. Ensure it is professional and appropriately dressed.

   Including details like date of birth, gender, and civil status. However, it's not strictly necessary, and you can choose to include them based on personal comfort and relevance.

3. **Language & Communication**
   Given our bilingual nature, indicating your proficiency in both Filipino and English is beneficial. If you are also familiar with regional languages or dialects (e.g., Cebuano, Ilocano), it is worth mentioning, especially if the job has regional interactions.

   Ensure your resume is free from jargon, especially if it is industry-specific. While English proficiency is high, clarity is vital to avoid any misunderstandings.

4. **Key Sectors & Industry Nuances**
   This industry is massive in our country. If applying within this sector, emphasize skills like communication proficiency, adaptability to different time zones, customer service aptitude, and technical proficiencies.

   With the growing IT industry, showcasing certifications, tech stacks you are familiar with, and specific projects can be a distinct advantage.

For roles in local companies, showcasing adaptability, understanding of the local market, and any previous experience with local businesses can be beneficial.

5. **Licenses & Certifications**
   For roles like engineering, architecture, nursing, or law, indicate if you have passed the respective board or bar exams. These are significant credentials.

   Highlight any courses or certifications that align with the job's requirements, especially if from recognized institutions or training centers.

6. **References & Connections**
   If you have references from within the country or from local professionals, it can be a plus point, providing localized validation of your skills and character.

   Filipino business culture places value on personal connections and referrals. If someone referred you to a position, and you have their permission, it might be beneficial to mention it.

Tailoring your resume for the Filipino market involves more than just listing skills and experiences. It is about resonating with local values, understanding market dynamics, and showcasing not just your capability, but also your fit within the Philippine professional landscape. As always, sincerity and authenticity are key; ensure that what you present aligns with who you are and what you genuinely bring to the table.

Common Keywords or Skills Sought After by Employers

In a globally connected market, employers look for a combination of universal skills and locally-relevant attributes in potential candidates. Being attuned to these desired competencies can enhance your resume's appeal. Let us explore the common keywords and skills employers in the Philippines typically value.

1. **Technical & Industry-Specific Skills**

   a. **BPO Competencies**
      Given the dominance of the BPO sector, skills such as *"Customer Service," "Technical Support," "Voice & Non-Voice Process,"* and *"Sales & Up-selling"* are often sought after.

   b. **IT & Tech Skills**
      With a burgeoning tech scene, mentioning proficiencies like *"Software Development," "QA Testing," "Tech Stack (specifics like Java, Python),"* and *"Web Development"* can be advantageous.

   c. **Finance & Business**
      Keywords like *"Account Management," "Auditing," "Financial Reporting,"* and *"Sales Forecasting"* are valued in the business sector.

2. **Soft Skills & Universal Competencies**

   a. **Communication Skills**
      Given the bilingual nature of many workplaces and the global clientele of numerous Filipino companies, *"Bilingual Communication," "English Proficiency,"* and *"Interpersonal Skills"* are crucial.

   b. **Adaptability**
      The dynamic nature of many sectors means *"Adaptability," "Flexibility,"* and the ability to handle *"Shift Work"* are often highlighted as desired traits.

   c. **Teamwork & Collaboration**
      Filipino workplace culture emphasizes *"Team Collaboration," "Cross-functional Teamwork,"* and *"Community Engagement."*

d. Leadership & Initiative
Keywords such as *"Leadership," "Project Management," "Mentoring,"* and *"Strategic Planning"* indicate a candidate's capability to lead and take charge.

3. Cultural & Contextual Skills

a. Cultural Sensitivity
An understanding and appreciation of Filipino culture and values can be a significant asset, especially for expatriates or those unfamiliar with the local context.

b. Local Languages
While English is widely spoken, proficiency in *"Tagalog"* or regional languages like *"Cebuano"* or *"Bikol"* can be a plus in roles that require local interaction.

c. Networking & Relationship Building
The importance of *"Relationship Management"* and *"Networking"* can't be overstated in the professional scene.

4. Personal Attributes & Work Ethic

a. Resilience & Perseverance
The spirit of "Bayanihan" and resilience in the face of challenges is highly valued. Keywords like *"Problem-solving," "Crisis Management,"* and *"Resilience"* resonate with employers.

b. Integrity & Honesty

"Trustworthiness," "Ethical Conduct," and *"Integrity"* are core attributes sought by employers across sectors.

   c. **Initiative & Proactiveness**
Being a *"Self-starter," showcasing "Proactiveness"* and *"Innovative Thinking"* can differentiate a candidate.

5. **Continuous Learning & Growth**

   a. **Up-skilling & Training**
In a rapidly evolving market, *"Continuous Learning," "Professional Development,"* and *"Certification"* are indications of a candidate's commitment to staying updated.

   b. **Mentorship & Training**
If you've been involved in *"Mentoring"* or *"Training"* others, it speaks to both your expertise and your commitment to collective growth.

When tailoring your resume for the job market, it is not just about inserting these keywords but contextualizing them within your experiences. Quantify achievements, provide concrete examples, and weave a narrative that showcases not just your skills but your understanding of the Filipino professional landscape. This holistic approach will make your application resonate more effectively with potential employers.

Common Mistakes & How to Avoid Them

Crafting a resume can be a meticulous task, and even small errors can have significant repercussions. Being aware of common pitfalls and their remedies ensures your resume portrays you in the best light. Let us explore these mistakes and how you can sidestep them.

1. **Generic Resumes**
   - **Mistake:** Using a one-size-fits-all resume for every job application, without tailoring it to specific roles.

- **Solution:** Customize your resume for each position you apply for. Highlight relevant skills and experiences that align with the job description. Use keywords from the job listing.

2. **Lack of Quantification**
   - **Mistake:** Listing duties without showcasing their impact or significance.

   - **Solution:** Quantify your achievements. Instead of saying *"Managed a team,"* say *"Led a team of 10 and increased department efficiency by 20%."*

3. **Too Lengthy or Too Short**
   - **Mistake:** Writing a resume that's overly lengthy and filled with unnecessary details or, conversely, too brief to adequately capture your qualifications.

   - **Solution:** Aim for conciseness while ensuring all crucial information is present. Fresh graduates or those early in their careers should typically have a one-page resume. Mid-level to senior professionals can stretch to two pages, or occasionally more if needed.

4. **Poor Organization & Layout**
   - **Mistake:** Presenting information in a haphazard manner or using a cluttered layout that's difficult to read.

   - **Solution:** Use a clean, professional format. Organize sections logically *(e.g., Contact Information, Objective, Experience, Education, Skills)*. Utilize bullet points for clarity, and ensure consistent formatting throughout.

5. **Grammatical & Typographical Errors**
   - **Mistake:** Overlooking spelling, grammar, or punctuation mistakes.

- **Solution:** Proofread your resume multiple times. Use tools like Grammarly. If possible, ask someone else to review it— they might spot errors you missed.

6. **Including Irrelevant Information:**
   - **Mistake:** Mentioning outdated or irrelevant work experiences, personal details, or skills.

   - **Solution:** Focus on your most recent and relevant experiences and skills. As a rule of thumb, experiences older than 10-15 years that don't add significant value can often be omitted.

7. **Using Passive Language**
   - **Mistake:** Writing in a passive voice or using weak verbs.

   - **Solution:** Use strong action verbs like "Achieved," "Managed," "Designed," or "Transformed" to start bullet points, making your contributions more dynamic and impactful.

8. **Over embellishment**
   - **Mistake:** Exaggerating achievements or responsibilities.

   - **Solution:** Be honest and authentic. Remember, during interviews or reference checks, embellishments can be uncovered and may jeopardize your credibility.

9. **Not Highlighting Transferable Skills**
   - **Mistake:** Overlooking skills gained in one role that can be beneficial in another, especially when changing careers or industries.

- **Solution:** Identify and emphasize transferable skills. For instance, project management, leadership, and problem-solving are valuable across various fields.

10. Omitting Online Presence

- **Mistake:** Not including professional online profiles or portfolios.

- **Solution:** If relevant, provide links to your LinkedIn profile, personal website, or online portfolio. Ensure any linked content is professional and mirrors your resume.

Avoiding these common mistakes requires a mix of attention to detail, an understanding of the job market, and self-awareness. Always approach your resume as an evolving document, updating and refining it based on feedback and the roles you're aiming for. With diligence and a keen eye, you can craft a resume that stands out for all the right reasons.

Crafting a standout resume is both an art and a science. As we have journeyed through this chapter, we have broken down each section of the resume, offering insights tailored to the unique cultural and professional nuances of the job market.

From the importance of presenting personal information in a culturally sensitive manner to highlighting achievements that resonate with local employers, we have provided a comprehensive guide to making a strong first impression. Moreover, by addressing common mistakes and their remedies, we have aimed to equip you with tools to ensure your resume shines with authenticity and professionalism.

In the next chapter, we will delve into the art of mastering job interviews, ensuring you are equipped not just to make a strong impression on paper, but also in person. Remember, your resume is the gateway to opportunities; make every word and detail count. Best of luck in your job-seeking journey!

CHAPTER 3:
MASTERING THE INTERVIEW

As the sun rises over the streets of Manila, many fresh graduates and job seekers find themselves preparing for one of the most fundamental steps in their career journey - the job interview. It is the moment where the neatly formatted text of your resume transforms into a living narrative, a space to humanize your achievements and directly connect with potential employers.

In our country interviews often go beyond assessing mere technical skills. They delve deep into understanding one's character, adaptability, and alignment with the organizational ethos. While a well-crafted resume might open doors, it is the nuances of the face-to-face interactions during interviews that ultimately secure job offers.

In this chapter, we will guide you through the intricacies of job interviews tailored for the market. From understanding common questions and cultural subtleties to effective negotiation and post-interview etiquette, we aim to equip you with strategies and insights that will help you stand out and resonate with Filipino employers.

Prepare to step confidently into that conference room, handshake ready, and vision clear. Let's unravel the secrets of acing job interviews!

Understanding the Filipino Interview Culture

The Filipino job interview process, like its global counterparts, is designed to evaluate potential candidates beyond what's written on their resumes. However, certain cultural nuances set the Filipino interview experience apart, with its unique blend of formality, warmth, and value-driven inquiry.

1. **Values and Respect**
    Always address your interviewer with respect, using titles such as "Mr." or "Ms." followed by their surname. This shows acknowledgement and courtesy.

The traditional mano, where one takes an elder's hand and places it against their forehead as a sign of respect, is primarily used in personal settings. However, it signifies the broader cultural importance of respect. In an interview, ensure you offer a firm handshake, maintain good posture, and use polite gestures.

2. **Warmth and Familial Atmosphere**
Do not be surprised if an interview starts with informal chit-chat about your journey, the weather, or even shared acquaintances. This is a way to break the ice and establish a connection.

In some cases, especially for higher-level positions, interviews might extend to lunch or dinner. This is not just about gauging your skills, but also understanding how you fit into the company's culture and team dynamics.

3. **Value-driven Questions**
While your skills are crucial, employers often place equal (if not greater) emphasis on your character, values, and how you resonate with the company's ethos.

Be prepared for hypothetical situations that test your moral compass, teamwork, and adaptability.

4. **Flexibility and Adaptability**
While tardiness is generally frowned upon in professional settings, be prepared for schedules that might not always be strictly adhered to. Nevertheless, always aim to be punctual for your interview.

Given the dynamic nature of many businesses, showcasing adaptability is key. You might be quizzed about handling unexpected challenges or adapting to changing scenarios.

5. **Endings and Follow-ups**
A simple gesture, but sending a thank you email or note after the interview shows appreciation and can leave a lasting positive impression.

Hiring decisions might sometimes take longer than expected. While it is appropriate to follow up, ensure you do so with patience and respect.

Understanding the interview culture goes beyond rehearsing answers. It is about connecting with interviewers on a deeper level, reflecting the intertwined professional and personal values intrinsic to the work culture. As you step into your interviews, remember that every interaction is an opportunity to showcase not just your expertise, but also the unique qualities you bring to the table. Next, we will delve into commonly asked questions and how best to approach them.

Preparing for the Interview - Setting the Foundation for Success

Interviews can be daunting, even more so in a culturally-rich and diverse environment. However, thorough preparation can dramatically alleviate anxiety, enhance confidence, and provide a distinct edge. Here's a deeper dive into how to lay the groundwork effectively before the interview.

Researching the Company - Unveiling the Layers of Your Prospective Employer

Stepping into an interview equipped with comprehensive knowledge about the company not only elevates your confidence but also signals your genuine interest and commitment to the role. But what does "researching the company" truly entail? Let's dive deeper.

1. **Company's Origins and Evolution**
   Understand the founding story of the company. When was it established? What challenges and milestones shaped its growth?

   How has the company evolved over the years? Has it expanded into new markets, introduced groundbreaking products, or undergone any significant rebranding?

2. **Mission, Vision, and Core Values**
   What is the company's mission? This usually pinpoints the problem they're striving to solve or the change they wish to effect.

The company's vision provides insights into its long-term goals and aspirations.

Core values often define a company's culture, decision-making process, and business ethics.

3. **Products, Services, and Key Clientele**
   Familiarize yourself with the company's product range or the services they provide. What sets them apart from competitors?

   Who are the primary consumers or users? Are there any key partnerships or collaborations worth noting?

4. **Industry Standing and Competitors**
   Is the company an industry leader, a challenger, or a newcomer?

   Identifying the main competitors offers insights into the broader industry landscape and where your prospective employer fits in.

5. **Recent News and Developments**
   These can be a treasure trove of recent accomplishments, product launches, or strategic shifts.

   If publicly listed, annual reports and financial statements can give an indication of the company's fiscal health and growth trajectory.

6. **Company Culture and Employee Sentiments**
   Websites like Glassdoor or JobStreet can provide employee reviews, which offer glimpses into the company's work environment, management style, and potential areas of improvement.

   The company's social media pages, especially LinkedIn, can offer insights into their events, initiatives, and employee highlights.

7. **Local Relevance**

Many companies blend global best practices with local traditions. Try to glean how the company integrates values and practices into its operations.

Given the strong community ties in Filipino culture, it is beneficial to know if the company engages in local CSR (Corporate Social Responsibility) initiatives for community projects.

Researching a company goes beyond mere surface-level understanding. It's a deep dive into its heart and soul, its challenges and triumphs, its past and envisioned future. Especially in our country, where personal connections are cherished, walking into an interview with a well-rounded understanding of the company can set you apart. As you embark on this research journey, see it as the first step in forging a meaningful connection with a potential new work family.

Dressing Appropriately - Ensuring Your First Visual Impression Resonates

In the heart of the Filipino job market, where tradition intertwines with modernity, dressing appropriately for an interview is more than just looking presentable. It is a statement of respect, understanding, and alignment with the company's culture. Here's an in-depth look at how to strike the right sartorial balance.

1. **Understand the Company's Culture**
   Traditional businesses such as banks, law firms, or governmental agencies, tend to favor a more formal dress code. In contrast, tech startups or creative agencies might lean towards a casual or smart-casual approach.

   Utilize company websites, social media pages, or even platforms like Glassdoor to glean insights into the workplace attire. Images from company events or regular workdays can be particularly revealing.

2. **When in Doubt, Go Neutral**

Neutral colors like black, white, navy, or gray are universally accepted and tend to appear polished and professional.

Extremely bright colors, flashy jewelry, or overly patterned outfits can be distracting. You want the interviewer to focus on you and your qualifications, not be overwhelmed by your attire.

3. **Dressing for the Tropical Climate**
   The Philippines is characterized by its humid and warm climate. Opt for breathable fabrics like cotton or linen. This ensures you remain comfortable without compromising on professionalism.

If you are wearing a blazer or suit, it is acceptable to remove your jacket once you have reached the venue and settled, especially if the weather is particularly sweltering.

4. **Grooming and Details**
   Ensure your hair is neat, clean, and styled conservatively. If you have long hair, consider tying it up to maintain a tidy appearance.

If you wear makeup, keep it understated and professional. Similarly, if you choose to wear perfume or cologne, ensure it is not overpowering.

Shoes should be polished and in good condition. Closed shoes are typically the safest bet for formal settings.

5. **Final Touches**
   While accessories can complement your attire, keep them minimal and elegant. For instance, a watch, simple earrings, or a modest necklace can enhance your overall look without being overly flashy.

Carry a professional-looking bag or briefcase that can hold your resume, necessary documents, and personal items neatly. Avoid overly large bags or those with loud designs.

Dressing appropriately for an interview is a harmonious blend of global professionalism with a touch of local sensibility. It's about projecting confidence, respect for the company's ethos, and a genuine understanding of the local context. As you stand before the mirror on interview day, ensure that your attire not only looks good but also feels authentic, allowing your genuine self to shine through. Remember, it's not just the outfit, but the individual in it that makes the lasting impression.

Understanding Common Questions - Navigating the Heart of the Interview

While each interview is unique, there are certain questions that consistently pop up across industries and roles. In our job market, where personal connections and values often intertwine with professional evaluations, it is paramount to anticipate and effectively address these common questions. Let us unpack them and outline strategies to tackle them.

1. "Tell me about yourself."

- **Objective:** This open-ended question is often used to kickstart the conversation and gauge your self-awareness and relevance to the role.

- **Strategy:** Begin with a concise overview of your professional journey, highlighting key roles, achievements, and transitions. Seamlessly integrate personal motivations or values that align with the position or the company's ethos.

- **Sample Answer:** *"Good Morning. I'm Maria, a marketing professional with over five years of experience in the tech industry. I started my journey as a junior marketing associate with TechSolutions, where I spearheaded digital campaigns, leading to a 25% increase in online engagement. Later, I transitioned to InnovateTech as a team lead, where I managed a group of ten and executed three major product launches. Beyond my professional achievements, I'm passionate about leveraging technology to connect with and serve local communities, which is one reason I'm so drawn to your company's community-driven initiatives."*

2. "Why did you choose to apply to our company?"

- **Objective:** Interviewers aim to assess if you have a genuine interest in the company and if your motivations align with its culture and goals.

- **Strategy:** Reflect on the company's mission, values, or any unique offerings that resonate with you. Whether it is their innovation, community involvement, or growth trajectory, pinpoint specifics that drew you in.

- **Sample Answer:** *"I've always admired ABC Corp's commitment to sustainable business practices, especially your recent initiative supporting local farmers in Mindanao. I believe in companies that don't just prioritize profit but also make a significant social impact. Joining a team with such values aligns with both my professional and personal aspirations."*

3. "Where do you see yourself in five years?"

- **Objective:** Understand your long-term ambitions and ascertain if they align with the company's potential growth opportunities.

- **Strategy:** While it is crucial to showcase ambition, ensure your answer aligns with the trajectory of the company and role. Emphasize skills you'd like to acquire, positions you aim to hold, or contributions you envision making.

- **Sample Answer:** *"In five years, I envision myself taking on more strategic roles, possibly as a department head, where I can further influence positive change and drive growth. I'm also keen on undergoing any leadership or technical training that would benefit the company and my growth within it. Ultimately, I aim to be in a position where I can mentor and uplift others, just as I was supported early in my career."*

4. "What are your strengths and weaknesses?"

- **Objective:** Gauge self-awareness, authenticity, and your potential fit for the role.

- **Strategy:**
  - **Strengths:** Highlight strengths that directly relate to the job description, providing real-life examples.

  - **Weaknesses:** Choose genuine areas of improvement but frame them positively. Highlight steps you're taking towards growth and how they might even be beneficial in certain scenarios.

- **Sample Answer:**
  - **Strengths:** *"One of my key strengths is adaptability. In my previous role, when our company shifted to a new digital platform, I was among the first to familiarize myself with it, eventually conducting workshops to train other team members."*

  - **Weaknesses:** *"As for weaknesses, I tend to be overly critical of my own work. While this ensures high-quality output, it sometimes means I spend too much time on details. I've been working on this by setting clearer benchmarks for quality and seeking feedback from peers to gain a more balanced perspective."*

5. "Why did you leave your last job?" or "Why are you looking for a new opportunity?"

- **Objective:** Understand your motivations for change and ensure they are not red flags.

- **Strategy:** Frame your answer positively. Focus on seeking new challenges, aligning more closely with your career goals, or wanting growth opportunities that the current role offers.

- **Sample Answer:** "I'm truly grateful for the learning and opportunities my previous company offered. However, I felt that I had reached a point where growth became stagnant. I'm seeking a new challenge and a chance to further expand my skill set, and I believe this role at your company provides the platform I'm looking for."

6. "How do you handle conflict or stress?"

- **Objective:** Ascertain your problem-solving abilities, emotional intelligence, and adaptability.

- **Strategy:** Use the STAR method (Situation, Task, Action, Result) to detail a real-life instance where you effectively managed a conflict or stressful situation.

- **Sample Answer:** *"In my previous role, (Situation) there was a situation where two team members disagreed on a project's direction. As the team lead, (Task) I facilitated a meeting where each could voice their concerns. (Action) I believe in open communication and active listening. (Result) By understanding each perspective and finding common ground, we were able to merge their ideas into a solution that benefitted the project. For stress, I find that taking short breaks and practicing mindfulness helps me maintain a clear and focused mind."*

7. "What can you bring to our team?" or "Why should we hire you?"

- **Objective:** Determine your unique value proposition and how it sets you apart from other candidates.

- **Strategy:** Align your skills, experiences, and personal qualities with the needs of the company and the specifics of the role. Provide concrete examples or scenarios where your contributions can make a significant impact.

- **Sample Answer:** *"With my blend of technical expertise and leadership experience, I believe I can offer both hands-on skills and strategic insights to your team. During my tenure at XYZ Company, I led a project that resulted* *in a 30% efficiency boost. I'm eager to bring that same drive and innovation to your team, especially since I resonate strongly with your company's mission of empowering local entrepreneurs."*

Understanding common interview questions is not just about rehearsing answers, but genuinely reflecting on them and tailoring them to the job at hand. In our country your authenticity, combined with thorough preparation, can create a memorable impression. As the old Filipino adage goes, "Sa taong may tiyaga, may nilaga" - to the person who perseveres, rewards await.

During the Interview - Mastering the Moment of Truth

Once you have walked through the door, every gesture, word, and interaction become an opportunity to create an impression. Here is a comprehensive guide on how to effectively navigate the interview itself, a crucial phase in the hiring process.

Body Language and Non-Verbal Cues

In many cultures, non-verbal cues can often speak louder than words. They provide a window into your confidence, sincerity, and enthusiasm.

1. **Eye Contact**
   Steady eye contact conveys confidence and attentiveness. However, ensure it feels natural and does not verge into staring. If there are multiple interviewers, shift your gaze to engage with each one, especially the person speaking.

2. **Handshake**
   Offer a firm (but not crushing) handshake. It should convey assertiveness and warmth. In the Filipino context, wait for the interviewer to initiate.

3. **Posture**
   Sit upright, which displays attentiveness and respect. Avoid

slouching or appearing too relaxed, which can be perceived as disinterest or arrogance.

4. **Facial Expressions**
A genuine smile can build rapport. Nodding occasionally indicates you're actively listening.

5. **Mirroring**
Subtly mirroring an interviewer's body language can foster rapport. But ensure it is subtle and does not feel mimicked.

Formulating Your Responses

Your answers should not only communicate your skills and experience but should resonate with the interviewer on a deeper, more genuine level.

a. **Be Concise**
Offer clear and structured answers. Avoid rambling or going off on tangents.

b. **Use the STAR Method:**
   - **Situation:** Describe the context.
   - **Task:** Explain your responsibility.
   - **Action:** Detail the actions you took.
   - **Result:** Highlight the outcomes, preferably quantifying them.

c. **Stay Authentic**
While it is essential to prepare, your answers should feel genuine, not rehearsed. Relate your answers to real experiences and emotions.

d. **Align with Company Culture**
Weave in aspects or values of the company into your responses when relevant, showing alignment and enthusiasm for their ethos.

Asking the Interviewer Question

Your questions can be as revealing as your answers, indicating your priorities, interests, and how deeply you have researched the company.

a. **Role-Related Questions**

"Can you describe a typical day for someone in this role?" or "What are the most immediate projects that need to be addressed by the person in this position?"

b. **Team Dynamics**

"Can you describe the team I'll be working with?" or "How does this team integrate with other departments in the company?"

c. **Company Culture**

"How would you describe the work environment here?" or "What do you think distinguishes this company from its competitors regarding culture?"

d. **Growth Opportunities**

"What does professional development look like here?" or "How does the company support ongoing learning and growth?"

An interview is a two-way street. While it is an opportunity for the employer to gauge your fit for the role, it is equally a chance for you to understand if the company aligns with your values and aspirations. Especially in our country, where relationships play a crucial role in professional settings, building genuine connections during the interview can pave the way for fruitful collaborations. Remember, each interaction, whether verbal or non-verbal, is a building block in the foundation of your potential relationship with the company.

After the Interview - Cultivating Professional Courtesy and Continued Engagement

Navigating the post-interview phase is just as crucial as the preparation and the actual interview. Here, nuances in approach, timing, and content can shape the interviewer's continued perception of you. Especially in a culture as relationship-centric, these gestures amplify your professionalism and genuine interest.

1. **Sending Thank You Notes**
    A well-crafted 'Thank You' note, sent post-interview, can leave a lasting impression. It's a reflection of your professionalism, gratitude, and continued enthusiasm for the role.

    -   **Timeliness**
        Ideally, send the note within 24 hours of the interview. This ensures your interaction is still fresh in the interviewer's mind.

    -   **Medium**
        A concise, well-crafted email is the most common medium, but a handwritten note can add a personal touch, especially for local or smaller companies.

    -   **Content**
        a. **Opening:** Begin by expressing gratitude for the opportunity to interview and their time.

        b. **Personal Touch:** Reference a memorable part of the conversation or something unique about the interview experience.

        c. **Reiteration:** Concisely restate your enthusiasm for the role and how you envision adding value to the team.

        d. **Closing:** Thank them again and express your eagerness to hear feedback or the next steps.

Sample Thank You Note:

"Dear Ms. Santos,

Thank you for the insightful conversation earlier today regarding the Marketing Manager position at ABC Corp. I genuinely appreciated your clarity on the challenges the team is currently facing and am excited about the potential solutions we discussed. Your emphasis on community-driven campaigns particularly resonated with my experience and passion.

I am eager to contribute to ABC Corp's mission and look forward to the possibility of collaborating closely with you and the team. Please let me know if there's any additional information you need from my side.

Thank you again for your time and consideration.

Warm regards,
Juan dela Cruz"

2. **Follow-Up Etiquette**
   The art of following up post-interview is a delicate balance between demonstrating continued interest and not appearing overly eager or impatient.

   - **Respect the Timeline:** If the interviewer provided a timeline for feedback, wait until that period elapses. If no timeline was given, a week is a standard waiting period before following up.

   - **Be Concise:** Your follow-up should be succinct, expressing gratitude again, reiterating interest, and seeking updates on the next steps or feedback.

   - **Stay Professional:** Regardless of the duration of the wait or any perceived delay, ensure your tone remains courteous and understanding.

Sample Follow-Up Email:

"Hello Ms. Santos,

I hope this email finds you well. I wanted to touch base regarding the Marketing Manager role I interviewed for last week. I remain deeply interested in the opportunity to join ABC Corp and contribute to the projects we discussed.

I understand how busy recruitment periods can be, so I appreciate the time and effort you're investing in this process. If there are any further details or documents you need from me, please do let me know.

Thank you once again for considering my application. I look forward to hearing from you soon.

Best regards,

Juan dela Cruz"

The period after the interview is one of reflection, anticipation, and continued engagement. By demonstrating professionalism, patience, and a genuine appreciation for the opportunity, you continue to solidify the positive impression you've made, cementing your place as a top contender for the role.

Turning Interviews into Opportunities

As we conclude this chapter, it is essential to reflect on the overarching theme: An interview is not just a process but an opportunity. It is a unique intersection where your journey meets the company's path, and together, the potential for a collaborative future is assessed.

The Filipino job market, with its deep emphasis on relationships, values, and community, offers a unique backdrop. Here, interviews transcend beyond mere qualifications and tap into genuine connections, shared values, and mutual growth visions. Your preparation, body language, responses, and post-interview engagements all come together to paint a holistic picture of who you are, both as a professional and as an individual.

Remember:

While spontaneity has its place, entering the interview room well-prepared sets a confident tone. Knowledge about the company, clarity about the role, and introspection about your journey and goals can be your strongest assets.

Genuine responses, true engagement, and authentic interest always stand out. In a world of rehearsed answers, let your sincerity shine.

From your attire to the thank-you note you send after the interview, every touchpoint builds upon the impression you leave behind.

Whether the outcome is a job offer or not, each interview offers learnings. Reflect on feedback, assess areas of improvement, and continuously refine your approach.

In the words of a Filipino proverb, *"Ang hindi marunong lumingon sa pinanggalingan ay hindi makakarating sa paroroonan."* Those who don't look back at where they came from will not reach their destination. As you step into future interviews, remember your journey, the lessons learned, the challenges overcome, and the aspirations that drive you forward.

Here is to turning each interview into a stepping stone towards your dream career in the vibrant and diverse Filipino job landscape. Mabuhay!

CHAPTER 4:
ACING PROBATION AND SECURING REGULAR EMPLOYMENT

Navigating the world of work is not just about securing a job offer; it is also about ensuring that your probationary period is a success, solidifying your place in the company for the long haul. This chapter delves into the intricacies of the probationary period in the Filipino context, offering strategies to not just navigate but excel in this critical phase.

UNDERSTANDING PROBATION
While the concept of probationary employment exists in many parts of the world, its application in our country reflects a unique blend of legal, cultural, and professional practices. Delving deeper into this critical phase of employment, we'll gain a more profound understanding of the intricacies involved.

Probationary Employment
The Filipino labor system recognizes the importance of allowing both employers and employees an evaluation period. Rooted in the Labor Code of the Philippines, the maximum duration for probation is typically six months, after which an employee is either regularized or their contract is terminated.

Why do companies have a probationary period?
Beyond being a legal provision, the probationary period serves practical and strategic purposes for employers.

Hiring involves costs, and making the wrong hire can be expensive. Probation allows companies to evaluate an employee's suitability before offering them regular status, which entails more benefits and protections.

This period lets employers train new hires, assessing their ability to internalize and apply new knowledge effectively.

Companies, where relationships are crucial, use this time to see if an employee fits well with the existing team and the overarching company culture.

From the employee's vantage point, it is a chance to understand the company, the role, and decide if this is where they envision their career growth.

What are they looking for?
Each company might have specific criteria, but several common themes persist:

a. **Skill Competency**
- This is not just about whether you can do the job, but how effectively and efficiently you perform your tasks. For instance, if you're in a sales role, it's about meeting targets and also building sustainable client relationships.

- Moreover, it is also about adaptability: how quickly do you grasp new tools, systems, or methodologies introduced?

b. **Cultural Fit**
- Filipino work culture places a high premium on "pakikisama" (camaraderie or getting along well with others). Can you work harmoniously with a team?

- Do you respect hierarchies while still fostering open communication?

- Are the company's values reflected in your actions and decisions?

c. **Attitude and Adaptability**
- The Filipino term "diskarte" captures this essence – a blend of resourcefulness, initiative, and adaptability, especially when faced with challenges.

- How do you handle feedback? In a culture that values "hiya" (a sense of shame or propriety), it's essential to accept feedback gracefully and use it constructively.

d. **Initiative and Drive**

- Companies appreciate employees who do not just wait for instructions but actively seek ways to contribute. This proactiveness is often seen as a sign of commitment and passion.

- Do you bring fresh ideas to the table? Are you enthusiastic about projects or initiatives? This reflects "sigasig" (zeal or enthusiasm) and is highly valued.

The probationary phase is not just a legal or procedural step; it's an opportunity for alignment – between the aspirations of an individual and the visions of a company. It's a dance of compatibility, commitment, and potential. Understanding its nuances helps in navigating this period with confidence and purpose, ensuring a fruitful journey ahead.

Strategies to Stand Out

Your probationary period is your canvas, and every action, big or small, contributes to the masterpiece you're painting. Standing out is not about grand gestures but consistent, valuable contributions and meaningful interactions. Here, we delve deeper into the strategies that can help you shine during this pivotal phase.

1. **Exceeding your job description**

   Merely meeting expectations can help you sustain your role, but to truly stand out, you need to exceed them. This is especially true in our work environment where dedication, initiative, and "malasakit" (genuine concern) are highly valued.

   Objective: It is about being an 'extra mile' employee, not just an 'as per the job description' one.

   Action Steps:

- **Identify areas of value addition**
  Perhaps there's a process within your department that's inefficient. Can you propose a solution? Or maybe there's a recurring problem that no one has addressed. Can you find its root cause?

- **Proactive sharing**
  Do not just keep your insights to yourself. Share them with your team or manager. Whether it is a new tool that can speed up a process or a market trend that could affect the business, your proactive nature will be appreciated.

2. **Volunteering for projects or assignments**
   In a culture that appreciates "bayanihan" (community unity and cooperation), volunteering showcases your commitment to collective goals.

   Objective: Be seen as a team player and someone who is willing to step up.

   Action Steps:

- **Stay Informed**
  Regularly liaise with colleagues or superiors to be aware of upcoming projects. Offer your services, even if it's something as simple as organizing a team event.

- **Balance is Key**
  While enthusiasm is great, ensure you do not take on more than you can manage. Quality should never be compromised for quantity. Remember the proverb, "Nasa Diyos ang awa, nasa tao ang gawa." (Mercy is in God's hands, action is in man's.)

3. **Building relationships and networking within the company**
   In our country, where relationships play a central role in both personal and professional life, networking is not just about

advancing one's career but also about building genuine connections.

Objective: Establish meaningful relationships that extend beyond professional requirements.

Action Steps:

- **Engage in Company Events**
  Whether it's the company's anniversary celebration or a team-building retreat, participate actively. These are excellent avenues to get to know colleagues outside of a strict work context.

- **Mentorship and Peer Learning**
  If you have a specific skill, consider conducting a workshop or training session. Alternatively, if there's an area you wish to improve in, seek out a mentor. This mutual exchange of knowledge not only benefits skill sets but also strengthens interpersonal bonds.

- **Regular Catch-ups**
  Initiate occasional coffee breaks or lunches with team members or people from other departments. A simple "Kamusta?" (How are you?) can pave the way for deeper conversations and connections.

Standing out during probation in the Filipino work environment is a blend of professional excellence and genuine interpersonal engagements. It's about showcasing your value while also valuing the community around you. With the right strategies, you can not only secure your position but also lay the foundation for a fulfilling and impactful career journey. Remember, in the end, it's about creating harmony between individual aspirations and collective growth.

Monitoring and Reviewing Your Performance

As you embark on your probationary journey, proactive monitoring and constant self-refinement can be your compass, guiding you towards successful regularization. Let's delve into strategies that can help you effectively assess, refine, and amplify your performance, especially in the relational and dynamic Filipino workplace.

1. **Setting up regular check-ins with your manager**
   In a country that values "pakikipagkapwa" (a sense of shared identity and community), open communication channels with superiors can be instrumental in building trust and clarity.

   Objective: Ensure you're on the right track, understand areas of improvement, and display genuine commitment to your role.

   Action Steps:
   - **Propose Scheduled Meetings**
     Rather than waiting for feedback, take the initiative to set up regular check-ins. It could be a quick 15-minute catch-up or a more extended session, depending on the depth of the discussion.

   - **Come Prepared**
     For each check-in, have a list of accomplishments, challenges faced, and questions or clarifications. This structured approach not only makes these sessions productive but also showcases your thoroughness.

2. **Seeking feedback actively**
   Feedback is a mirror reflecting your performance. Actively seeking it shows your willingness to grow and improve.

   Objective: Gain insights into your performance from multiple perspectives and refine accordingly.

   Action Steps:
   - **Broaden Your Feedback Net**
     While your manager's feedback is crucial, peers, subordinates,

or cross-departmental colleagues can offer varied perspectives. A collaborative task or a project might have given them insights into your working style, which could be invaluable.

- **Constructive Feedback**
  When requesting feedback, specify that you are looking for constructive criticism. The Filipino cultural trait of avoiding direct confrontation might make some hesitant but emphasizing that it's for your growth can make them more forthcoming.

- **Implementation**
  Act on the feedback received. If someone pointed out an area of improvement, work on it, and during the next interaction, subtly highlight the change. It shows that you value and act on input.

3. **Continuous self-improvement and skill development**
   In the ever-evolving professional landscape, staying updated is not just a bonus but a necessity. The Filipino value of "kasipagan" (diligence) can be your guiding star here.

   Objective: Keep enhancing your skillset, ensuring you remain a valuable asset to the company.

   Action Steps:

   - **Skill Upgradation**
     Identify areas in your field that are emerging or where you feel a gap. Enroll in online courses, attend workshops, or read up on the latest trends.

   - **Network**
     Attend industry seminars, webinars, or workshops. Not only do you gain knowledge, but you also build connections that could be beneficial in the long run.

- **Application**
  Implement what you learn. If you have picked up a new technique or tool, find ways to incorporate it into your work. It not only boosts productivity but also displays initiative.

Your probationary period is a continuous journey of performance, feedback, and refinement. By being proactive, open to feedback, and committed to continuous learning, you lay the foundation for a robust professional trajectory. In our country, where personal relationships, commitment, and growth are deeply interwoven, these strategies can be your roadmap to success. Remember, "Ang taong masipag, daig ang malakas" – A diligent person will win over a strong person. Let diligence, reflection, and growth guide your probationary journey.

From Probationary to Permanent - Crafting a Legacy of Excellence

As we bring this chapter to a close, let us reflect upon the heart of the matter: The probationary phase is not just a trial or an evaluation. In the dynamic and relational landscape of the Filipino workplace, it's an opportunity to sow the seeds of trust, competence, and genuine commitment.

Probation is more than just about assessing technical fit; it's about cultural immersion, adaptability, and building "kapwa" (shared identity) with your colleagues and the organization's vision. It's about melding the intricate tapestry of your skills, aspirations, and values with the broader mission of the company.

Here's what to remember:

- **Proactivity Over Passivity**
  Take charge of your growth. From scheduling check-ins to seeking feedback, be the captain of your ship.

- **Continuous Learning**

The world and workplace are in a constant state of flux. Equip yourself, stay updated, and always be on the lookout for avenues of growth.

- **Relationships Matter**
  Beyond tasks and targets, focus on the human aspect. Forge genuine relationships, respect the cultural nuances, and be a team player.

- **Self-Reflection**
  Amidst all external feedback, make time for introspection. Celebrate your achievements, acknowledge areas of improvement, and set goals for the future.

The Filipino proverb, "Bago mo hanapin ang kahinaan ng iba, hanapin mo muna ang kahinaan mo" translates to, "Before you point out the weaknesses of others, look for your own first." This journey is as much about self-awareness as it is about external validation.

As you navigate this crucial phase, know that every day is a step towards solidifying your place, not just as an employee, but as a valuable member of a community. Here's to your journey from probationary to permanent, marked by growth, excellence, and "malasakit" (genuine care). Mabuhay!

CHAPTER 5:
SUCCESS STORIES – FROM ASPIRATIONS TO REALIZATIONS

Behind every professional success are challenges, learnings, efforts, and triumphs. Success stories serve as powerful testaments to the reality that with the right mindset and strategies, anyone can navigate the waters of the Filipino job market and rise to prominence. In this chapter, we dive into anecdotal experiences of individuals who, with their determination and adaptability, have made an indelible mark.

The following names are fictional, but the experiences indicated in every success story in this chapter are real and are based on the stories of my former employees in the past years.

a. The Power of Perseverance

Maria, a fresh graduate from a provincial university, moved to Manila with dreams of joining the IT industry. Facing rejections initially due to her unfamiliar alma mater, she did not falter. Instead, she enhanced her portfolio by taking on freelance projects and attending workshops. During her probation at a top tech firm, she regularly sought feedback and even proposed process improvements which were later implemented. Today, Maria leads a team of developers and is an advocate for continuous learning.

Takeaway: Never let rejections deter you. Continuous self-improvement and proactive engagement can turn obstacles into stepping stones.

b. Turning Setbacks into Comebacks

Liza joined a marketing agency, and within the first month, a campaign she led did not produce the expected results. Instead of getting disheartened, Liza took this as a learning opportunity. She requested an in-depth feedback session, learned from her missteps, and led two successful campaigns subsequently, all within her probationary period.

Takeaway: Mistakes are inevitable. It is your response to them that defines your trajectory.

c. Beyond the Role

Rafael, a finance executive, believed in going beyond his numerical tasks. He volunteered for CSR initiatives, organized team-building activities, and even conducted financial literacy sessions for his peers. By blending his expertise with his passion for community, Rafael became an indispensable part of his organization within just a few months.

Takeaway: Your role is a starting point. Melding professional expertise with personal passions can create a legacy.

While each journey is unique, underlying themes of proactivity, continuous growth, and genuine interpersonal connections prevail. As you chart your path, let these stories be a beacon, reminding you that success is a blend of skill, attitude, and heart.

Embracing Your Journey in the Job Market

As we turn the final pages of this guide, let us pause to reflect on the journey we have undertaken together. From crafting a standout resume to navigating the intricate dance of interviews, and from acing probationary challenges to drawing inspiration from success stories – we have delved deep into the job market's multifaceted landscape.

The Philippines, with its unique blend of Eastern and Western influences, its vibrant culture of "kapwa" (shared identity) and "bayanihan" (community spirit), and its undying resilience, offers a job market like no other. Here, success is not just measured by titles or salaries but by relationships built, values upheld, and the impact created.

Key Takeaways:

- Whether it is your resume, interview, or probationary period, being prepared and genuine sets the foundation for lasting success.

- The world is ever-evolving, and so should you be. Embrace learning opportunities, be it through courses, feedback, or self-reflection.

- Engage sincerely, understand cultural nuances, and build a network of trust and collaboration.

- Challenges will arise. Embody the Filipino spirit of "diskarte" (resourcefulness) and "bangon" (rising after setbacks) to navigate through them.

- From a successful interview to a well-executed project during probation, celebrate your achievements, no matter how big or small. They shape your professional narrative.

YOUR UNIQUE JOURNEY

While this guide provides a roadmap, remember that everyone's journey is unique. Your experiences, challenges, and triumphs will be your own, and that is what makes them special. Let our values of community, diligence, and authenticity guide you, but also let your individuality shine through.

NAVIGATING THE JOB MARKET LEXICON

Congratulations on taking the leap from the world of academia to the dynamic realm of professional work! As you set foot in this new chapter, you'll not only face challenges and opportunities but also a sea of terms and jargon that might seem a little daunting at first. Fear not! Just as you've mastered the terminologies of your academic field, you can quickly familiarize yourself with the lingo of the job market.

The transition from being a student to a full-fledged professional involves understanding not only the intricacies of your chosen profession but also the broader language of the job world. Some of these terms might already be familiar, while others could be entirely new.

Why is this important? Well, knowledge is power. Understanding these terms will help you navigate job listings, interviews, and workplace discussions with confidence. It's like being handed a map in a new city – knowing the main streets and landmarks makes the journey a lot smoother.

In the following section, we've collated essential terminologies that you might encounter in your early career. They're grouped by relevance, making them easier to understand and remember. And to make things even more relatable, we've peppered in real-world examples that bring these terms to life.

Dive in, and soon enough, you'll find yourself speaking the language of professionals with the same ease as your native tongue!

1. **Resume/CV (Curriculum Vitae):** A document highlighting an individual's education, work experience, skills, and achievements, typically used to apply for a job.

2. **Cover Letter:** A written document that accompanies a job application, which introduces the applicant and explains why they are suitable for the job.

3. **Job Description (JD):** An outline provided by employers that describes the responsibilities, qualifications, and duties of a particular position.

4. **Soft Skills:** Non-technical skills that relate to how you interact with others, such as communication, teamwork, and problem-solving.

5. **Hard Skills:** Specific, teachable abilities or knowledge sets, such as data analysis or computer programming.

6. **Networking:** The act of meeting and connecting with professionals in your industry to gain insights, opportunities, and contacts.

7. **Onboarding:** The process of integrating a new employee into a company and familiarizing them with the company culture, policies, and their role.

8. **Probationary Period:** A trial period during which an employer can evaluate a new employee's performance before deciding on permanent employment.

9. **Benefits Package:** Compensation over and above the salary, which may include health insurance, retirement plans, paid vacation, bonuses, and more.

10. **Exit Interview:** A meeting between an employee leaving a company and a representative from human resources to discuss the employee's reasons for leaving and overall experiences at the company.

11. **Performance Review:** An evaluation of an employee's work performance, usually conducted annually or semi-annually.

12. **Mentorship:** A relationship where an experienced individual (mentor) provides guidance, advice, and support to a less experienced individual (mentee).

13. **Freelance:** Working on a contract basis for a variety of companies, as opposed to working as an employee for a single company.

14. **Remote Work:** Performing one's duties outside of the traditional office setting, typically at home.

15. **Salary Negotiation:** The process of discussing and determining the compensation package for a job position.

16. **Transferable Skills:** Abilities and knowledge that can be used in different job roles or industries. For instance, leadership and project management are transferable across various sectors.

17. **Portfolio:** A collection of work samples showcasing an individual's skills and accomplishments, often used in creative industries.

18. **Recruitment Agency:** A company that specializes in finding and recruiting candidates for job vacancies on behalf of other companies.

19. **Glass Ceiling:** An unofficial barrier that prevents certain groups, often women and minorities, from advancing to the top levels of a profession.

20. **Work-Life Balance:** The equilibrium between personal life and career work, and the efforts to ensure one doesn't overshadow the other.

21. **Reference:** Someone who can vouch for your qualifications for a job, often a previous employer or colleague.

22. **Temporary Position:** A job role that is not permanent and usually has a set end date.

23. **Full-time vs. Part-time:** Full-time jobs typically require 40-48 hours per week, while part-time jobs require fewer hours.

24. **Moonlighting:** The act of holding a secondary job, often in the evening or during spare time, in addition to one's primary job. It can be to pursue a passion, develop a skill, or simply to earn extra income.

25. **Non-compete Clause:** A contract provision that prevents an employee from working for or becoming a competitor for a certain period after leaving their job.

26. **Telecommuting:** Working from a location outside of the traditional office environment, usually from home, using telecommunication tools.

27. **Gig Economy:** A labor market characterized by short-term contracts or freelance work as opposed to permanent jobs.

28. **Professional Development:** Activities, courses, or events that help professionals gain new skills or knowledge in their field.

29. **Compensation Package:** The combination of salary and other benefits (health insurance, retirement benefits, paid vacation, bonuses, stock options) that an employee receives from an employer.

30. **Internship:** A temporary position, often for students or recent graduates, which provides real-world experience in a particular industry or field.

31. **Traineeship:** Similar to an internship, but more focused on training the individual for a specific role or job.

32. **In-house:** Refers to activities or employees that are within, or a part of, the organization itself, as opposed to being outsourced.

33. **Outsourcing:** Contracting work out to an external company or individual rather than doing it in-house.

34. **Headhunter:** A type of recruitment agent who specializes in sourcing candidates for specific, often high-level, positions.

35. **Severance Package:** Compensation and benefits given to an employee when they leave a company, especially during layoffs or terminations.

36. **Flextime:** A scheduling system that allows employees to choose, within limits, their own working hours.

37. **Stock Options:** A benefit in which employees are given the option to buy company stock at a reduced price.

38. **Affirmative Action:** A policy or program designed to redress historic injustices against specific groups by giving them certain privileges in employment and education opportunities.

39. **Equal Employment Opportunity (EEO):** Laws, regulations, and practices that ensure that all candidates have a fair chance at employment, prohibiting discrimination based on factors like race, color, religion, sex, or nationality.

40. **Employee Retention:** Efforts and strategies companies use to keep their employees and reduce turnover.

41. **Whistleblower:** An individual who exposes illicit activities or wrongdoing within their organization.

42. **Constructive Dismissal:** When an employee resigns because their employer's behavior has become intolerable, effectively forcing them to leave.

43. **Upskilling:** The process of learning new skills, especially as technology evolves or job functions change.

44. Downsizing: The act of reducing the number of employees, usually for the purpose of saving costs.

ACQUIRING ESSENTIAL GOVERNMENT MANDATES

For fresh graduates in the Philippines, stepping into the professional world involves a few more steps than just crafting a resume. Before fully immersing oneself in the workforce, it's crucial to be registered with certain government agencies. This ensures you're compliant with the nation's labor and taxation laws. Here's a guide to help you navigate through these requirements:

1. **Social Security System (SSS):**
   - **Purpose:** Provides social insurance for workers in the private, professional, and informal sectors.

   - **Requirements:** Birth certificate, any valid ID, personal details.

   - **Procedure:** Visit the nearest SSS branch or use the online SSS portal to fill in the E-1 form. Once completed, submit the form along with the necessary documents.

2. **Philippine Health Insurance Corporation (PhilHealth):**
   - **Purpose:** Provides health insurance coverage and ensures affordable healthcare services.

   - **Requirements:** Two 1x1 ID pictures, photocopy of a valid ID, and a filled-out PhilHealth Member Registration Form (PMRF).

   - **Procedure:** Head to the nearest PhilHealth office, submit the PMRF form along with your pictures and valid ID. Once processed, you'll receive a PhilHealth ID and number.

3. **Pag-IBIG Fund (Home Development Mutual Fund):**

- **Purpose:** Offers housing loans to members and serves as a savings system.
- **Requirements:** At least one valid ID and a filled-out Member's Data Form (MDF).

- **Procedure:** Visit a Pag-IBIG branch, submit the MDF with your ID. After verification, you'll be provided with a Pag-IBIG MID number.

4. **Tax Identification Number (TIN) from the Bureau of Internal Revenue (BIR):**
   - **Purpose:** Essential for taxation purposes.

   - **Requirements:** Birth certificate, valid ID, and any document indicating your address.

   - **Procedure:** Visit the nearest BIR office, fill out the BIR Form 1901 for self-employed or mixed-income individuals, or BIR Form 1902 for local employees. Submit with required documents. After processing, you'll be given your TIN.

Key Points to Remember:
- Always bring original and photocopies of your documents.

- It's advisable to keep a personal file containing all these documents and IDs for future use.

- Some employers assist new hires with these registrations as part of their onboarding process, but it's beneficial to be familiar with the procedure.

ADDITIONEAL ESSENTIAL REQUIREMENTS FOR FILIPINO PROFESSIONAL

While registrations with the major government institutions lay the foundation for your professional life, there are other essential requirements that employers might ask for, depending on the nature of the job. Here is a guide to help you navigate through these:

1. **Cedula (Community Tax Certificate):**
   - **Purpose:** Proof of payment of community tax.

   - **Requirements:** Personal appearance, valid ID, and recent photo.

   - **Procedure:** Visit your local city/municipal hall. Provide the necessary details and pay the corresponding tax. The cedula will be issued to you immediately.

2. **Police Clearance:**
   - **Purpose:** Verifies that you have no criminal record in your municipality.

   - **Requirements:** Barangay Clearance, valid ID, recent photo, and payment of the necessary fee.

   - **Procedure:** Apply at the local police station. After paying the fee, your name will be checked against local police records. If cleared, the certificate will be issued.

3. **NBI Clearance:**
   - **Purpose:** Ensures you have no criminal record nationwide.

   - **Requirements:** Any two valid IDs, personal appearance for photo and fingerprint capturing.

- **Procedure:** Either apply online via the NBI Clearance website or walk in to an NBI Clearance Center. Pay the fee, and once your identity is verified and you have no records, the clearance will be issued.

4. **Health Card (for food industry workers):**
   - **Purpose:** Ensures workers handling food are free from contagious diseases.

   - **Requirements:** Medical examination results, valid ID, and fee.

   - **Procedure:** Visit the local health center or city/municipal hall, undergo a medical exam (often including a chest x-ray and blood test). Once cleared, you pay the fee and receive your health card.

5. **Medical Examinations with 'Fit to Work' Certificate:**
   - **Purpose:** Assures employers that you're physically and mentally fit for the job.

   - **Requirements:** Depending on the job, you might need chest x-rays, blood tests, drug tests, psychological tests, etc.

   - **Procedure:** Attend a clinic or hospital specified by your employer. After undergoing the necessary tests, a physician will issue a 'Fit to Work' certificate if you pass.

Key Points to Remember:

- Fees for these requirements vary by location and are subject to change. It is advisable to check current fees before applying.

- Always bring original documents and keep photocopies for your records.

Some clearances and certificates have expiration dates. Ensure you renew them as needed.

Being proactive and prepared with these requirements not only speeds up your job application process but also demonstrates responsibility and dedication to potential employers.

A FINAL NOTE

To all the fresh graduates and young professionals reading this: Embrace the journey with enthusiasm and hope. The job market, with all its intricacies, is ready for you. Equipped with the insights from this guide and fueled by your aspirations, step confidently into the next chapter of your career.

Maraming salamat for embarking on this journey with me. Here's to your success, growth, and the incredible stories you'll craft in the Filipino professional world. Mabuhay ka!

ABOUT THE AUTHOR

Mac Aldio Belenzo, CHRA is an experienced HR practitioner, and currently works in a company in the hospitality industry. Born and raised in Sampaloc, Manila, Philippines, Mac has always been captivated by the complex balance of tradition and modernity that defines the Filipino professional landscape.

Having graduated from Far Eastern University with a degree in Bachelor of Science in Psychology; currently taking Master of Research and Development Management in University of the Philippines – Open University and having obtained the Certified Human Resource Associate conferment from the Human Resource Association of the Philippines (HREAP), Mac quickly ascended the corporate ladder, thanks to a keen understanding of local corporate distinctions combined with global best practices. Earlier this year, Mac took part in a program sponsored by the local government unit (LGU) in his province. He served as a mock interviewer for over 500 graduating students from a community college there. After the mock interviews, he provided advice and tips on how to effectively answer interview questions. This book is a culmination of those experiences and the wisdom he gathered along the way.

With a firm belief that everyone possesses the potential to shine, Mac seeks to empower the next generation of professionals to carve their niche in the evolving job market.

Made in the USA
Las Vegas, NV
11 January 2024

84205668R00046